REAL TAPAS

Santa Maria # 65

- Chips de yuca 375
- Anchoas con pan con tomate 675
- Hojaura de atún con cebolla tierna y aceite de oliva 675
- Cecina de León 775
- Ensalada de castañas y calabaza y queso feta 675
- "Ravellons" con apio y mantequilla de cacahuete en ensalada 775
- Empanadillas de setas y pato confitado 415
- Ancas de rana marinadas con salvia y gengibre 675
- Guiso de caracoles con tortilla japonesa 650
- Sushi de verduras con salvia 925
- Maki de aguacate y pepino 750
- Maki de gamba y lechón rebozado 1100
- Sushi variado 2500
- Huevos de codorniz escalfados con pisto y christoma 450
- "Ravellons botó" a la plancha 900
- Alcachofas guisadas con berengenas 625
- Tortitas de avellana 675
- Salteado de arroz integral con shitake, esparragos y judías 625
- Truchas de río con acelga, champiñones y cecina 575
- Bacalao con bomato y encurtidos 775
- .... de ...... con manzana 875
- .... de avellana, col lombarda 875
- Pechuga de pato con pera y pimienta sichuan 800 y patata 850
- Albas de pollo tandoni 475
- Surtido de quesos 675

* A partir de 5 comensales
sólo se sirve menu degustación *

= Postres =

- Piña colada con chupa-chups 450
- Helado de caki, plumb-cake y toffe 675
- Manzana reineta con bizcocho de frutos secos y helado de chocolate 675
- Trufas de chocolate 375

REAL
TAPAS

FIONA DUNLOP

75 authentic recipes to share

Photography by Jan Baldwin

MITCHELL BEAZLEY

An Hachette UK Company
www.hachette.co.uk

First published in Great Britain in 2002 by Mitchell Beazley,
an imprint of Octopus Publishing Group Ltd, Endeavour
House, 189 Shaftesbury Avenue, London WC2H 8JY

This edition published 2013 by Octopus Publishing Group

Distributed in the US by Hachette Book Group USA, 237 Park
Avenue, New York, NY 10017 USA

Distributed in Canada by Canadian Manda Group, 165
Dufferin Street, Toronto, Ontario, Canada M6K 3H6

ISBN   978 1 84533 824 4

Publisher Alison Starling
Art Director   Jonathan Christie
Photographer   Jan Baldwin
Recipe Translator Ana Sims
Project Editor   Jo Wilson
Assistant Production Manager Lucy Carter
Indexer   Diana LeCore
Commissioning Editor for original edition
Becca Spry
Editors for original edition Georgina Atsiaris, Jamie
Ambrose, Hattie Ellis

Printed and bound in China

CONTENTS

INTRODUCTION

In the last decade or so, tapas have conquered the world, radiating from their Hispanic source to tease the taste buds of anyone in search of a generous snack to accompany a glass of wine. Yet such pan-national culinary clones are mere shadows of the real thing, found only in Spain. Racy flavors, high contrasts, generous doses of virgin olive oil, ultrafresh ingredients, fearless use of offal, and obsessive use of salt cod or cured ham—these are just some of the hallmarks of Spanish tapas.

Naturally enough, much tipsy speculation has taken place over the origins of tapas. The word *tapa* ("lid"), from *tapar* ("to cover"), allegedly refers to slices of cheese or ham used to cover glasses of sherry in the hot, insect-infested bars of Andalucía. From these prosaic beginnings, so the story goes, came the tradition of serving small portions of bar food free with a glass of beer, wine, or sherry. An alternative theory originates from the thirteenth century, when the Castilian king, Alfonso X, surrendering to doctor's orders to recuperate from an illness, spent long days in bed, sipping small glasses of restorative wine accompanied by reduced portions of food. His recovery was so painless that a royal decree was announced, ordering taverns to serve wine only if accompanied by a snack.

Yet another, more down-to-earth theory equates tapas with the routines of the rural working day, tiding over appetites and boosting energy in a climate not always conducive to huge meals or hard labor. Pre- or post siesta, grazing was the way to go for Spain's agricultural masses.

Whatever their starting point, tapas have moved on and are now inextricably linked to the Spanish way of life. They have generated the *tapeo* (tapas bar-hopping): a unique, mobile institution that brings swarms of families out onto the streets when the heat of the day has passed, to stroll, gossip, and stop for a drink—and, naturally, a tapa or two.

The continuation of the habit is ensured by the presence of many generations, from grandpas to babies, while floors scattered with used paper napkins, cocktail sticks, olive pits, mussel shells, and the odd errant anchovy all point clearly to the lip-smacking gusto of the activity.

There is no sitting around at isolated tables at an appointed hour, victim to the whims of restaurant staff. The tapeo is something else: spontaneous, convivial, and informal, yet it occurs within customary time slots on a year-round basis. Different, the Basques opt for the word *poteo*, a derivative of *potes* ("pots" or "jars"), from which wine or cider was drunk.

Traditionally, each bar cooked up only one tapas specialty, and this enforced peripatetic snacking on a population only too happy to prolong its voluble socializing. Drunkenness is rare; while spirits and decibels soar, excess alcohol is rapidly absorbed by sporadic feeding. You still find unique house specialties in smaller towns, but today's bars are more likely to chalk up a list of tapas and *raciónes* ("rations," or larger portions) of the day. Again, the exception comes from the Basque region, where tapas are replaced by *pintxos* (or *pinchos*), finger snacks that resemble French canapés and scale new heights of diversity and elaborateness.

All this is part of the late 20th century awakening and post-Franco bounce, when sophisticated *nueva cocina* (new cuisine) galvanized chefs into producing ever-more-inventive juxtapositions of ingredients and flavors. The initial impetus came from France via the Basques, and has since conquered local cuisine from Seville to Barcelona, Madrid to Salamanca. This renaissance has inspired most of the recipes in this book, which were created by chefs in search of exciting gastronomic departures. Glutinous bean stews and sad-looking *picadillo* (diced vegetable) salads, move on! Few tapas are universal in Spain; local produce is paramount. The "rural-folkloric revival" (a term coined by anthropologist

T. Seppilli in 1992) is galloping ahead, highlighting local delicacies (anything from blood sausage, legumes, or organic cured ham to a snail or a quail) that may even be produced in a specific valley or village. This is nurturing a taste for quality. One exception is the ubiquitous *ensaladilla* ("little salad" or Russian salad), a tapa of canned vegetables smothered in mayonnaise that just won't go away. For foreigners bemused by its similarity to 1960s airline food, the ensaladilla does raise questions as to the gastronomic discernment of this tapas-consuming nation. But then the French still snack on *croque monsieur*, so why not? There has to be some sort of atavistic yearning at work here. Mayonnaise itself appears again and again, whether straight out of a jar or as garlic-enhanced *aioli*.

The gastronomic euphoria of the last two decades goes hand in hand with Spain's newfound prosperity and awareness of the outside world. These, in turn, have led Spaniards to a greater pride in their own roots and cultural identity. Regionalism is king and labels of regulated quality, are proliferating; once used only for the country's wines *Calificada (DOCa)* for Rioja, this type of quality control now extends to foodstuffs such as white beans or suckling pigs.

Today's well-traveled chefs are concocting fusion food that harks back to Spain's cosmopolitan history. The wheel turns full circle to reintegrate Arab contrasts of flavors originally brought to the country by the Moors. Similarly, the Roman art of fish preserving never went away. The basis of Spanish cuisine continues to be dominated by New World products: the potato, tomato, fava bean, and chili pepper. Add to this Phoenician, Greek, and Jewish influences and you soon come to realize that by tasting Spanish tapas, you are tasting a good part of the globe, yet the cuisine was developed long before the term "fusion food" was coined.

VERDURAS

VEGETABLES

ALCACHOFA CON ACEITE DE OLIVA NEGRA
ARTICHOKE HEARTS WITH BLACK-OLIVE OIL

This ultra simple recipe is light and delicious, yet looks like a work of art.

FOR 8 TAPAS

- ½ lb. pitted black olives
- ½ cup extra-virgin olive oil
- 8 artichoke hearts, cooked, or canned and well-drained

Prepare the black-olive oil by mixing the olives and oil in a blender until the olives are finely chopped.

Just before serving, place the artichoke hearts on a plate and pour the black-olive oil over them.

ENSALADA DE CALABAZA,

PUMPKIN, CHESTNUT, FETA CHEESE, AND POMEGRANATE SALAD

FOR 8 TAPAS

6 oz. lamb's lettuce (or mâche), torn into
    bite-sized pieces

1 small, curly endive (escarole), coarse leaves
    removed and torn into bite-sized pieces

1 bunch of watercress

½ lb. feta cheese, broken into small cubes

1½ spring onions, thinly sliced

seeds of 1 pomegranate

½ lb. chestnuts, cooked, peeled, and halved

¾ lb. pumpkin, julienned

1 fl. oz. white wine vinegar

½ cup extra-virgin olive oil

salt and pepper to taste

The happy collusion between Asian influences and Catalonia's fantastic array of autumnal produce has inspired this salad tapa. Every autumn, chestnut-roasters take root in the streets of Spain, while market stalls acquire the Dali-esque shapes and colors of abundant squash varieties. In this recipe, you can vary or simplify the lettuce types, as the main interest lies in the balance of fresh pumpkin, chestnuts, feta, and sweet pomegranate seeds.

Arrange all the salad ingredients in eight small bowls (or one large one).

Make the vinaigrette by whisking the white wine vinegar and olive oil together and seasoning with the salt and pepper.

Dress the salad, toss lightly, and serve immediately.

LEEKS WITH SUMMER VEGETABLE VINAIGRETTE

For centuries, leeks were relegated to support roles in Castilian cooking, but they are back on center stage, particularly in the province of Segovia, where they are extensively cultivated. In this recipe, the colorful vegetable vinaigrette that covers the stacked white leeks makes for a particularly refreshing tapa.

FOR 6 TAPAS

12 slim leeks, white portion only, stripped of outer layer and root

1 tbsp. olive oil

1 onion, finely chopped

1 small red pepper, finely chopped

1 small green pepper, finely chopped

¼ lb. gherkins, rinsed of vinegar and finely chopped

¼ lb. capers, rinsed of vinegar, brine, or salt and finely chopped

2 small green tomatoes, finely chopped

½ cup extra-virgin olive oil

2 tbsp. white wine vinegar

salt to taste

1 bunch watercress

At least one hour before serving, cook the leeks in plenty of salted boiling water and one tablespoon of olive oil for 12 minutes. Drain, cool, and cut the leeks in half lengthwise.

Prepare the vegetable vinaigrette by mixing together the onion, peppers, gherkins, capers, and tomatoes, then coating with the olive oil, white wine vinegar, and salt.

Just before serving, put a bed of watercress on a plate and stack the leeks on top. Cover with the chopped vegetables.

PATATAS AL POBRE

POOR MAN'S POTATOES

There are endless variants to this recipe in southern Spain, some of which include red or green peppers. If you want to incorporate peppers, they should be deseeded and sliced and added immediately after the onion and before the potatoes.

FOR 6 TAPAS

10 tbsp. olive oil, for frying

2 large Spanish onions, sliced into rings

6 medium-sized, firm potatoes, peeled and sliced

salt to taste

1 tbsp. sherry vinegar

3 cloves of garlic, finely chopped

In a heavy frying pan, heat two tablespoons of oil and fry the onions for 10 minutes, stirring occasionally, until they are golden.

Add the remaining oil, allow to heat, then add the potatoes and cook for another 15 to 20 minutes, until they are tender. Season with salt and drain off any excess oil.

Mix the vinegar and garlic together, pour over the potatoes, then stir. Serve immediately.

ESPINACAS CON GARBANZOS A LA ANDALUZA

ANDALUCÍAN-STYLE SPINACH WITH CHICKPEAS

This classic Andalucían dish has traveled to tapas bars all over Spain, such is its earthy appeal. The spinach and chickpeas are, surprisingly, Moorish imports.

FOR 6 TAPAS

2 lb. 4 oz. fresh spinach, washed and destalked

¼ cup olive oil

10 oz. cooked chickpeas 1 tsp. ground cumin

salt and pepper to taste

3 cloves of garlic

1 slice of bread, fried in oil until golden

1 tsp. red wine vinegar

2 tbsp. water

1½ tsp. paprika

In a covered saucepan, cook the spinach, using only the water that clings to it after washing, for about four minutes, until it is wilted. Cool, then press out the excess water. Chop roughly.

Sauté the spinach in the oil over a low heat for about one minute. Add the chickpeas, cumin, salt, and pepper, and stir thoroughly.

Pound the garlic and fried bread with a mortar and pestle or chop them in a blender until fine. Add to the spinach and mix well.

Add the vinegar, water, and paprika, and cook over a low heat, stirring constantly, for about one minute. Serve at once in individual earthenware dishes.

PATATAS ALIÑADAS
SEASONED MASHED POTATOES

This is a delicious tapa created from the simplest ingredients. Seasoned mash is generously bathed in extra virgin olive oil from Andalucía, often premier oils from Baena or Priego de Cordoba (mixing Hojiblanca and Picudo varieties). Don't worry if you can't find it, but use the best substitute you can find. In typical Manuel fashion, this is a delicious tapa created from the simplest ingredients.

FOR 6 TAPAS

2 lb. 4 oz. new potatoes, scrubbed

3 spring onions, white part only, finely chopped

3 green peppers, finely chopped

½ cup plus 2 tbsp. extra-virgin olive oil

3 tbsp. white wine vinegar

salt and pepper

few sprigs of Italian parsley

Cook the potatoes in boiling, salted water for about 20 minutes or until they are tender.

Remove the skins and mash the potatoes, then push the mashed potatoes through a sieve or potato ricer. Add the onions and peppers.

Slowly add the oil and vinegar, beating until the potatoes are thick and creamy. If more oil and vinegar is necessary, add in proportions of three parts oil to one part vinegar.

Season with salt and pepper and serve immediately on small plates, with a parsley garnish.

PATATAS A LA IMPORTANCIA
POTATOES OF GREAT IMPORTANCE

This is another example of Spain's sustaining peasant snacks, made from basic ingredients with strong flavors.

FOR 4 TAPAS

2 large potatoes, peeled and cut into
  ½-inch slices

¼ lb. cooked ham, in thin slices

¼ lb. French Chaumes or Port
Salut cheese, cut into thin slices

salt to taste

beaten egg, for coating

all-purpose flour, for coating

1 cup olive oil, for frying

FOR THE SAUCE

2 tbsp. olive oil

7 cloves of garlic, thinly sliced

1 bunch of Italian parsley, chopped

2 tbsp. all-purpose flour

1 cup white wine

Between two potato slices, place one slice of ham and one slice of cheese. Season with salt. Dip in the beaten egg, then in the flour, and fry in hot oil until the potato is golden and fully cooked. Remove.

To make the sauce, heat the oil in a frying pan. Add the garlic and sauté until tender. Add the parsley and stir. Blend in the flour, stirring until the mixture has thickened. Take the pan off the heat and stir constantly, adding the wine a little at a time.

When the wine has been added, put the pan back on the heat and bring to a boil, stirring. Simmer for five minutes. Pour the sauce over the potatoes and serve immediately.

FRITURA DE LA HUERTA
FRITATA OF GARDEN VEGETABLES

The choice of vegetables is yours but, as always, follow the seasons for the best results. Obvious alternatives to those used in this recipe are green and red peppers. The light batter produces a crisp coating that resembles tempura.

FOR 4 TAPAS

2 oz. onion, cut into thin rings

2 tbsp. flour

2 oz. cauliflower, separated into florets and briefly cooked

1 egg, beaten

½ cup dried breadcrumbs

2 oz. eggplant, peeled and cut into small cubes

1 tbsp. milk

olive oil, for frying

salt to taste

Dip the onion rings in flour. Dip the cauliflower first in the flour, then in the egg, then in the breadcrumbs. Moisten the eggplant cubes in milk and then coat with flour.

Heat about 2½ inches of olive oil in a frying pan and, when hot, cook the vegetables separately. Drain on paper towels and then add salt to taste.

Arrange attractively on a plate and then serve promptly.

AJO BLANCO
CHILLED ALMOND SOUP

This soup, invented by the Moors to counteract Andalucía's scorching-hot summers, can look divinely minimalist served in white bowls and garnished with floating muscatel grapes. It makes a refreshing change from some of Andalucía's stronger flavors, as the almond flavor is extremely subtle.

FOR 4 TAPAS

8 oz. blanched almonds

3 cloves of garlic

about 1½ cups fresh white breadcrumbs

2¼ cups water

2 tbsp. sherry vinegar

salt to taste

6 tbsp. olive oil

8 muscatel (or similar) grapes

extra-virgin olive oil, to serve

Finely grind the almonds and garlic in a blender. Add the breadcrumbs, water, vinegar, and salt, and blend for two minutes.

Slowly add the olive oil, while continuing to blend, until you have a creamy liquid. Refrigerate for at least one hour.

Serve in individual soup bowls, with a grape or two and a light drizzle of extra-virgin olive oil in each one.

RATATOUILLE WITH QUAIL EGGS

Pisto originated in La Mancha, but soon conquered the south and became Andalucía's answer to Provençal ratatouille: a mixture of braised Mediterranean vegetables served with a fried egg. When preparing the vegetables, keep them in separate dishes so that you can easily add them successively.

FOR 4 TAPAS

6 green peppers, diced

1 large onion, diced

olive oil

1 lb. 2 oz. eggplant, peeled and diced

1 lb. 2 oz. zucchini, diced

1 lb. 2 oz. tomatoes, diced

salt and pepper to taste

4 quail eggs

In a large pan, sauté the peppers and onion in olive oil until tender. Add the eggplant and sauté for five more minutes. Add the zucchini and sauté for three more minutes.

Add the tomatoes, lower the heat, and simmer for 20 minutes. Season five minutes before the cooking time has ended.

Quickly fry the quail eggs in some olive oil.

To serve, heap generous portions of ratatouille on individual serving plates and top with a fried egg.

CHAMPIÑONES EN SALSA VERDE
MUSHROOMS IN PARSLEY SAUCE

Serve this tapa in a shallow terra-cotta dish—the perfect foil for the juicy mushrooms and their green sauce. This dish is quite delicious and the ingredients are available all year round.

FOR 8 TAPAS

½ **cup virgin olive oil**

6 **cloves of garlic, minced**

½ **red chili pepper or 2 dry cayenne peppers**

2 **lb. 4 oz. fresh white mushrooms, cleaned, halved, or quartered, depending on their size**

salt and pepper to taste

1 **tbsp. all-purpose flour**

FOR THE SAUCE

2 **cloves of garlic, finely chopped**

leaves from a small bunch of Italian parsley, finely chopped

salt and pepper to taste

1 **cup white wine**

Mix the garlic, parsley, white wine, salt, and pepper for the sauce in a blender. Set aside.

Pour the olive oil into an ovenproof casserole or heavy-based saucepan, add the garlic, and sauté over a low heat until tender. Add the chili pepper and mushrooms and increase the heat. Cook, stirring constantly, until the juice has been drawn out of the mushrooms. Season and continue to simmer on a moderately high heat for about 10 minutes, stirring occasionally, until the juice has evaporated.

Sprinkle the flour over the mushrooms and stir to blend well. Remove from the heat and slowly add the sauce ingredients, stirring it in thoroughly. Return the dish or pan to the heat and bring to a boil, stirring constantly. Simmer for five minutes, until you have a fairly thick sauce. Serve hot.

HUEVOS Y QUESOS

EGGS & CHEESES

TORTILLA DE PATATAS
POTATO TORTILLA WITH WHISKY SAUCE

FOR 6 TAPAS

½ cup olive oil

2 lb. 4 oz. potatoes, peeled and cubed

3 eggs, beaten

salt and pepper to taste

FOR THE WHISKY SAUCE (SALSA DE WHISKY)

3 cloves garlic, finely sliced

2 tbsp. olive oil

2tbsp. butter

1 tbsp. lemon juice

1 tbsp. whisky

2 tbsp. strong beef stock

There are hundreds of variants of tortilla across every region of Spain, but the *tortilla de patatas* is a real Spanish classic. This Sevillian version comes doused in a whisky sauce.

Heat the olive oil in a deep frying pan. Cook the potatoes in the oil over a very low heat for about 15 minutes, until they are tender but not brown.

Meanwhile, make the sauce. Sauté the garlic slices in the olive oil until they are tender. Add the butter, lemon juice, whisky, and beef stock. Cook over a low heat, stirring occasionally, for 15 minutes, until reduced.

In a bowl, mix the potatoes with the beaten eggs, and season to taste. Pour the mixture back into the frying pan and cook over a low heat for three to four minutes. When the tortilla is firm but not dry, cover the frying pan with a plate of equal size and, grasping the plate and pan, flip the tortilla out onto the plate.

Carefully slide the tortilla back into the pan and cook for another three minutes to brown the other side.

Turn out onto a serving plate and cool for at least five minutes. Slices can be served hot or at room temperature, covered with the whisky sauce. Garnish with a whole pickled garlic clove and herbs such as snipped chives, and chopped parsley.

TORTILLA CACHONDA
TRICKY TORTILLA

You hardly know this is an omelette, albeit Spanish-style, when it appears on Pep's lengthy bar because it is covered in a deliciously thick layer of creamy aioli—hence the dish's name. Cut a slice, however, and you know you're in the realm of tortilla. If you have a small frying pan, so much the better to make individual tortillas, but one large tortilla works equally well.

FOR 4 TAPAS

olive oil, for frying

¼ lb. chorizo or other spicy cured sausage, thinly sliced

2 medium potatoes, cooked, peeled, and sliced

½ small onion, finely chopped and sautéed until soft

3 eggs, beaten

salt and pepper to taste

2 tbsp. aioli

FOR THE AIOLI (GARLIC MAYONNAISE)

2 cloves of garlic

sea salt

1 egg yolk

½ cup olive oil

lemon juice to taste

salt and white pepper to taste

Make the aioli by crushing the garlic with a little sea salt. Stir in the egg yolk and beat thoroughly. Add the olive oil a drop at a time, continuing to beat, increasing the stream of oil as more becomes incorporated. You should end up with a thick, creamy mixture. When you've added all the oil, add the lemon juice, then salt and pepper to taste. Cover and refrigerate immediately.

To make the tortilla, heat one tablespoon of olive oil in a small frying pan and sauté the chorizo quickly, until just browned. Add the potatoes and onion and stir.

In a bowl, mix the chorizo, potatoes, and onion with the eggs. Put two tablespoons of oil into the pan and pour the mixture back into it. Cook over a low heat for three minutes. When the omelette is firm but not dry, cover the skillet with a flat plate and flip it over to turn the omelette out onto the plate. Slide the omelette back into the pan and cook for three minutes to brown the other side. Cool for five minutes, then serve with a layer of aioli.

BERENJENA CON QUESO
EGGPLANT AND CHEESE FRITTERS

This, Casa Pali's flagship tapa, is easy and quick to prepare. It can even be half-cooked in advance and refried at the last minute. Your guests will need small knives and forks to devour it. For extra flavor, you can drizzle some liquid honey over the aubergines before serving.

Season each slice of eggplant with salt. For each tapa, place one slice of cheese between two slices of eggplant.

Dip each sandwich of eggplant in egg and then flour. Fry in a little olive oil over a medium heat until golden on both sides. Serve hot.

FOR 4 TAPAS

- - - - - - - - - - - -

4 thin slices of tangy, easy-to-melt cheese, such as Chaumes, cut to fit the eggplant

8 thin slices of eggplant

salt to taste

2 beaten eggs, for coating

all-purpose flour, for coating

olive oil, for frying

PUERROS CON CREMA DE QUESO

CREAM CHEESE AND LEEK TOASTS

The traditional Castilian leek is dominant in this tapa, and perfectly complemented by the cream cheese.

FOR 4 TAPAS

3 oz. cream cheese

¼ cup sunflower oil

2 tbsp. milk

2 slices of white bread, crusts removed, cut in half

4 very fine leeks, cut in half horizontally, cooked, and cooled

8 capers

Mix the cheese, oil, and milk in a blender until creamy.

Toast the bread and place two leek halves on each piece.

Cover with the cheese sauce and garnish with a caper at each end.

Place under the broiler for one minute. Serve hot.

TORTILLA DE AJETES, HABITAS Y JAMÓN
YOUNG GARLIC, FAVA BEAN, AND HAM OMELETTE

This is a another flavorful twist on the classic Spanish potato tortilla, and is a dish that should always be served at room temperature.

FOR 4 TAPAS

2 oz. (about 2 cloves) tender young garlic, finely chopped

olive oil, for frying

2 oz. small, young fava beans, cooked

2 oz. serrano ham (or prosciutto), cut into thin strips

3 eggs, well beaten

salt and pepper to taste

In a medium-sized frying pan, sauté the garlic in a little olive oil until tender and golden. Add the beans and ham strips and stir until warm.

Add the eggs and seasoning and cook for three to four minutes to form a firm but juicy omelette. Cool to room temperature, cut into triangular slices or squares, and serve.

QUESO DE CABRA FRITO CON MIEL
FRIED GOAT CHEESE WITH HONEY

This is an exquisite, though rich, nueva cocina tapa. The hot goat cheese is a delicious match for the cold, caramelized onions. The honey should not be too highly flavored, as this would drown the more subtle cheese, and it must drizzle easily. The parsley is optional, but adds a splash of color to this minimalist plate.

FOR 4 TAPAS

3 medium-sized, sweet red onions, very finely sliced

3 tbsp. olive oil, for frying

4 tbsp. sugar

5 oz. cylindrical goat cheese

1 beaten egg

all-purpose flour

2 tbsp. honey

1 tbsp. finely chopped parsley

2 chive stalks

Prepare the garnish several hours before serving. Fry the onions in the oil over a low heat until very soft; it will take about 20 minutes. Drain off the excess oil and add the sugar. Stir until the sugar and onions are blended and the sugar has caramelized (about eight minutes). Cool and refrigerate.

About 30 minutes before serving, form four equal balls of goat cheese. Dip each in the egg, then in the flour, and fry in just enough oil to cover the bottom of a frying pan. Turn carefully to lightly brown all sides. Drain on a paper towel.

Put the caramelized onions in the center of a serving plate and evenly space the fried cheese balls around it. Drizzle with honey, then sprinkle parsley over the top and add a crisscross of chives. Serve immediately.

QUESO CON MEMBRILLO
CHEESE AND QUINCE

Saltiness and sweetness combine in
this traditional Spanish tapa. You
could experiment with different
cheeses from the mountains of
Asturias, source of dozens of types
mixing cow, ewe and goat milk, but
ultimately, however, nothing can beat
the satisfying tanginess of traditional
Manchego.

FOR 6 TAPAS

6 slices of Manchego cheese

3 slices country bread

quince paste

dried fruit, almond flakes, and toasted pine
    kernels, to serve

Place a piece of Manchego cheese on a
half-slice of bread.

Place a smaller wedge of quince paste on top
of the cheese. Serve on a board with the dried
fruits and seeds.

CARNES

MEATS

FOIE GRAS, ZUCCHINI, AND BITTER-ORANGE TOASTS

This is an unusual combination of flavors, yet the end result is a wonderfully rich and luxurious tapa. Miguel uses *foie mi-cuit*, a superior version of foie gras with a more subtle flavor, but if you can't find it, use regular foie gras.

For each tapa, sandwich a quarter of the foie gras between two zucchini slices. Brush with a little oil and broil for three minutes on each side.

Toast the bread. Spread a little marmalade on each slice and top with a zucchini and foie gras sandwich. Sprinkle with pepper and serve at once.

FOR 4 TAPAS

1 oz. foie gras

8 (⅛-inch) zucchini slices

olive oil

4 slices of French bread, cut diagonally

1 tbsp. bitter-orange marmalade

black pepper to taste

MUSLOS DE POLLO A LA MIEL
HONEY-BAKED CHICKEN THIGHS

This simple though beguiling recipe is dominated by the sweet honey— a Moorish legacy. Enjoy it in summer with dry white wine or dry sherry.

To prepare the honey sauce, combine all the ingredients, except the chicken thighs, in a saucepan. Mix well and bring to a boil. Reserve.

Place the chicken thighs in a roasting pan, pour on the sauce, and bake in a preheated oven at 350°F for about 35 minutes or until the chicken is dark, glossy, and cooked. Serve hot.

FOR 4 TAPAS

1 cup honey

about ½ cup butter

1 tsp. curry powder

1½ tsp. dry mustard

about ⅓ cup ketchup

8 chicken thighs

HABITAS CON JAMÓN EN CONCHA DE ACHICORIA

IBERIAN HAM AND FAVA BEAN SALAD

Pulses are big in central Spain, but this recipe has chosen to limit their quantity while emphasizing their visual appeal.

If using fresh fava beans, cook them in a little water for anything from 2 to 5 minutes, until tender (the younger they are the less cooking time they need). If using dried fava beans, soak them overnight, then cover them with fresh water and cook for 1 to 1½ hours, until tender. In both cases, once the beans have been drained and cooled slip them out of their skins.

Place the radicchio leaf in ice water for about 15 minutes, until it brightens and stiffens.

Pour a little oil in a medium-sized frying pan. Add the garlic and cook slowly over a low heat, until just golden. Add the ham strips, heat for 10 seconds, then add the fava beans. Season with salt to taste. Cook, stirring occasionally, until the beans are hot.

While the beans are frying, remove the radicchio leaf from the ice water, pat dry, and place on a serving plate. Fill the leaf with the beans, allowing some to overflow onto the plate. Sprinkle with parsley and serve hot.

FOR 4 TAPAS

½ lb. fava beans, cooked or 5oz of dried fava beans

1 large, very fresh radicchio (Italian chicory) leaf

olive oil, for frying

2 cloves of garlic, finely sliced

¼ lb. Iberian ham or baked ham, thickly sliced and cut into thin strips

salt to taste

2 tsp. finely chopped parsley

GARBANZOS CON BUTIFARRA NEGRA

CHICKPEAS WITH BLOOD SAUSAGE IN GARLIC AND PARSLEY

This classic Catalan tapa is the result of a wonderful combination of creamy chickpeas, sweet raisins, meaty blood sausage, and crunchy pine nuts— a truly Hispanic assault on the senses!

Put two tablespoons of olive oil in a saucepan over a low heat, then sauté the onion until it is just tender. Add the garlic, parsley, raisins, and pine nuts, and mix well.

Add the blood sausage andchickpeas and heat through, stirring all the time. Season with salt and pepper. Transfer to a serving platter, drizzle with olive oil, and serve at once.

FOR 4 TAPAS

- - - - - - - - - - - - -

olive oil

½ large onion, thinly sliced

1 garlic clove, finely chopped

2 tbsp. finely chopped fresh parsley

1 oz. golden raisins, soaked in hot water for 15 minutes and drained

a sprinkling of pine nuts

5½ oz. blood sausage, fried and coarsely chopped

14-oz. can cooked chickpeas

(garbanzo beans), drained

salt and pepper to taste

HIGADO DE PATO CON PERA Y PIMIENTO SZECHUAN

DUCK LIVER WITH SWEET PEARS AND SZECHUAN PEPPER

Duck liver is the creamiest and the smoothest liver you can get, and in Paco Guzman's recipe, it is perfectly combined with freshly poached pears and a hint of mild Szechuan pepper. Use chicken's liver if duck's liver isn't available.

FOR 4 TAPAS

2 tbsp. sugar

5 tbsp. water

2 pears, peeled and thinly sliced

5½ oz. duck liver, cut into four slices

1 tbsp. olive oil

4 tsp. Szechuan pepper

Mix the sugar and water in a pan and heat until the sugar has dissolved. Add the pears and poach until they are just tender. Drain, reserving the liquid, and set them aside. Bring the liquid to a boil and boil until syrupy. Return the pears to the liquid and stir well.

Sauté the liver in the oil until it is lightly browned on each side. Arrange on a plate.

Spoon the pears and syrup over the liver. Grind the pepper and sprinkle on top. Serve immediately.

TENTEMPIÉ TRADICIONAL SEGOVIANO CON PATATAS NUEVAS

TRADITIONAL FRIED SEGOVIAN PORK AND POTATO

This hearty Segovian dish has strong rural and wintry overtones straight from the heart of Old Castile. It traditionally filled empty peasant stomachs with an artful combination of leftover pork and seasonal new potatoes. Quick to prepare, it is more than just a substantial tapa, as it works equally well for brunch or as an evening snack.

FOR 6 TAPAS

1 lb. 2 oz. new potatoes, peeled and thinly sliced

1 large onion, thinly sliced

olive oil, for frying

4 eggs

4-oz. piece of roast pork, cut into 1-inch-wide strips

salt and pepper

4 slices of fried French bread

Fry the potatoes and onion in plenty of olive oil over a low heat for about 20 minutes; they should be just tender. Drain the excess oil from the frying pan and continue to brown the vegetables lightly.

Break the eggs directly over the potatoes and onions. Add the pork, season well, and stir to mix all the ingredients together. Cook until the eggs are just set. Serve immediately, accompanied by the fried bread.

FRIED ASPARAGUS, HAM, AND CHEESE BUNDLES

The classic marriage of ham and cheese is made more interesting by the texture and subtle flavor of the asparagus. Riojans love canned asparagus spears, so for authenticity's sake, don't worry about finding the fresh variety (but use it if you prefer the extra crunch). This is one of Logroño's rare tapas that needs a knife and fork.

FOR 4 TAPAS

4 thin slices of mild, easy-to-melt cheese, such as French Port Salut or mild cheddar

4 asparagus spears, cooked until just tender

4 thin slices of cooked ham

beaten egg, for coating

all-purpose flour, for coating

olive oil, for frying

Place one slice of cheese and one asparagus spear on each slice of cooked ham, then carefully roll into a cylinder.

Dip the ham rolls in the egg and then the flour, then fry them in a little hot oil until they are golden brown. Serve immediately.

PIMIENTOS RELLENOS DE MORCILLA

RED PEPPERS STUFFED WITH BLOOD SAUSAGE

Spain offers endless varieties of blood sausage, but other countries are less inventive, so find the best you can. The combination of the dark blood sausage and the fresh red pepper is quintessentially Spanish, and Albur has raised this classic dish to new heights by adding basil, ginger, and pine nuts.

FOR 8 TAPAS

8 small red peppers (preferably piquillo—can be canned) or 4 red bell peppers

olive oil, for brushing

½ lb. blood sausage, preferably from León

1 egg, beaten

2 leaves of fresh basil, finely chopped

2 tbsp. butter

2 tbsp. all-purpose flour

½ cup milk

3 oz. chickpeas, cooked, drained, and pureed

½ tsp. ground ginger

salt and pepper to taste

1 tbsp. pine nuts

If you are using canned piquillo peppers, just drain them. If you are using raw peppers, brush them with olive oil and broil them until they are tender, partly black, and blistered. Set aside until cool enough to handle, then peel off the skins, halve, deseed, and set aside.

In an ungreased frying pan, fry the blood sausage, breaking it into small pieces with a wooden spoon as it cooks. Remove from the heat, add the egg, and stir until the egg has set. Add the basil and stir. Set aside.

In a saucepan, melt the butter, add the flour, and stir to form a roux. Cook for two minutes. Remove from the heat and slowly add the milk a little at a time, beating well after each addition. Put the pan back on the heat and bring to a boil, stirring until the sauce has thickened. Add the chickpea puree, ginger, and seasoning. Simmer for four minutes. Pour into a shallow ovenproof dish.

Fill the pepper halves with the blood sausage mixture, arrange them on top of the chickpea sauce, and sprinkle with pine nuts. Cook at 350°F for 10 minutes and serve.

CROQUETAS DE JAMÓN
HAM CROQUETTES

Competition to make the best ham croquettes is ruthless. All over Spain, some sad attempts and a few delectable ones are created. The Casa Pali version is a rare bird, as it achieves the perfect blend of reassuring creaminess and smoky ham flavor in a deliciously crisp outer coating.

FOR 6 TAPAS

4 tbsp. butter

¾ cup all-purpose flour

1¾ cups milk

1 small onion, finely chopped

1 tbsp. olive oil

2 oz. Serrano ham, finely chopped

salt and pepper

2 beaten eggs, for coating

fine, dry breadcrumbs, for coating

½ cup olive oil, for frying

Melt the butter in a frying pan. Add the flour and stir for three to four minutes, until well-blended, to form a roux. Remove from the heat and add the milk slowly, a bit at a time, mixing until smooth. Put the pan back on the heat and bring the milk up to boiling point, stirring constantly. The mixture should become very thick. Turn the heat to low and cook for about five minutes, stirring occasionally.

Sauté the onion in the olive oil until it is soft but not browned. Add the ham.

Stir the onion and ham into the white sauce and season well with salt and pepper. In a lightly greased 8 × 4-in. pan, spread the mixture to about a one-inch thickness and chill for at least two hours.

When cool, cut the chilled mixture into small bars, then use your hands to shape each bar into a little cylinder.

Coat each croquette with egg and breadcrumbs. Pour about three inches of olive oil into a pan and heat. Fry the croquettes, a few at a time, until they are golden brown on the outside and warm and cooked in the middle. It's a good idea to test one to check whether your oil is at the correct temperature.

Drain on a paper towel and either serve hot or at room temperature.

JAMÓN, ALCACHOFA Y HABITAS CON ALI OLI

HAM, ARTICHOKE, FAVA BEAN, AND AIOLI TOASTS

This tapa and the following ones can be made together, offering alternative flavors but sharing the aioli topping. They are both simple to prepare, and the coating of aioli hides the ingredients for a flavorful surprise.

Toast the bread, and on each slice place a quarter of the ham, folded to fit the bread, three fava beans, and a slice of artichoke heart.

Cover each tapa with a generous amount of aioli and dust with paprika before placing under a very hot broiler for 15 to 20 seconds.

FOR 4 TAPAS

4 slices of French bread, cut diagonally

¼ lb. Serrano ham

12 fava beans, cooked and drained

1 artichoke heart, cooked, drained, and sliced into four pieces

¼ cup Momo's aioli (garlic mayonnaise—see page 29)

paprika

JAMÓN, SALMÓN, HABITAS CON ALIOLI Y QUESO

HAM, FAVA BEAN, SMOKED SALMON, AND AIOLI TOASTS

Ham and smoked salmon work well together here, united by the alioli disguise. Although not from Spanish waters, salmon has conquered Spanish palates in recent years.

FOR 4 TAPAS

4 slices of white bread

1 slice of cooked ham, chopped

12 fava beans, cooked and drained

¼ cup Momo's aioli (garlic mayonnaise— see page 29)

1 slice of smoked salmon, chopped

Toast the bread, and on each slice place a quarter of the ham, folded to fit the bread, and three fava beans.

Cover each tapa with a generous amount of aioli, then garnish with a little smoked salmon at each end before placing under a hot broiler for 15 to 20 seconds.

CALDERETA DE CORDERO

LAMB STEW

This dish reflects the fact that lamb is still king in many parts of northern Spain. The stew could easily be served as a main dish if the quantity were increased and potatoes served with it. Note that the mixture of lamb cuts adds to the flavor and texture.

FOR 6 TAPAS

2 tbsp. olive oil

1 lb. 9 oz. lamb (half leg meat and half shoulder meat), cut into chunks

seasoned all-purpose flour, for coating

1 large onion, coarsely chopped

1 red and 1 green pepper, deseeded and coarsely chopped

4 cloves of garlic, chopped

½ red chili pepper, deseeded and chopped

1½ tsp. hot, smoked Spanish paprika (pimentón de la Vera)

1 tsp. fresh thyme

1 tsp. fresh rosemary

1 bay leaf

1¾ cups dry white wine

salt and pepper to taste

Heat the olive oil in a casserole dish. Dip the lamb chunks in flour, then brown them on all sides in the hot olive oil. Remove the lamb with a slotted spoon.

Put the onion, peppers, garlic, and chili in the same casserole dish and cook until tender.

Stir in the paprika, then add the lamb, herbs, and white wine. Season and bring to a boil. Immediately turn down the heat very low, cover the pan, and cook the lamb gently for about an hour or until the meat is well done and very tender. Serve in a shallow earthenware dish.

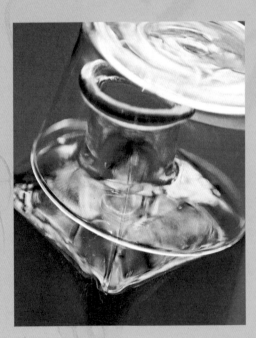

ALBÓNDIGAS DE CORDERO A LA HIERBABUENA

MINTED LAMB MEATBALLS

Although Spain offers numerous variants on the meatball theme, these are arguably some of the tastiest in the entire country.

FOR 6 TAPAS

1 lb. 2 oz. lamb, ground or finely chopped

salt and pepper to taste

3 cloves of garlic, finely chopped

1 tbsp. chopped, fresh mint

2 small eggs, beaten

4 tbsp. soft breadcrumbs

½ cup dry sherry

1 tbsp. olive oil, for sautéing

FOR THE SAUCE

2 onions, finely chopped

1 clove garlic, finely chopped

1 tbsp. olive oil, for sautéing

1 cup thick tomato paste

1 tbsp. dry sherry

water, for thinning

Combine all the meatball ingredients, except the olive oil, in a large bowl and mix well. Form the meat into one-inch balls and sauté in oil until lightly browned on all sides. Drain on paper towels and set aside.

In the same pan, sauté the onions and garlic for the sauce in olive oil until soft. Add the tomato paste and sherry and simmer for 10 minutes. Remove from the heat.

In a blender, puree the sauce until smooth, adding a little water if it's too thick. Return the sauce to the sauté pan and add the meatballs. Bring to a boil and cook over a medium heat for about 10 minutes. Serve hot.

CHORIZO AL VINO

SPICY SAUSAGE IN RED WINE

In the north of Spain, chorizo is often cooked in cider, but this recipe uses red wine instead of cider to create a warmer dish. This makes an excellent wintry tapa to accompany glasses of good Rioja.

FOR 4 TAPAS
- - - - - - - - - - - - - -

1 lb. 4 oz. chorizo orother spicy sausage

1½ cups dry red wine

1 bay leaf

Place the sausage in a frying pan with the wine and bay leaf. Cover and cook over a low heat for 10 to 15 minutes, or until the wine has been slightly reduced.

Remove the sausage from the pan and cut it into half-inch slices. Return the slices to the wine and stir. Serve in individual earthenware dishes with chunks of French bread.

BISTEC TARTAR DE MICHELE
SPICY STEAK TARTAR

The palate is under a happy assault from this spicy tapa, with its fiery mix of onion, chilies, capers, and hot-pepper sauce.

FOR 6 TAPAS

4 tbsp. finely chopped parsley

4 mild chili peppers, deseeded and finely chopped

1 small onion, finely chopped

2 oz. capers, well rinsed

1 lb. 2 oz. sirloin steak, finely chopped

6 drops hot-pepper sauce

salt and pepper to taste

extra-virgin olive oil to taste

¼ cup Dijon herb mustard

In a bowl, mix together the parsley, chilies, onion, and capers. Add the finely chopped sirloin and mix well.

Sprinkle with hot-pepper sauce, salt, pepper, and oil and mix to combine all the ingredients. Heap on a platter or on individual plates and serve with the herb mustard.

PINCHOS MORUNOS
SPICY PORK KABOBS

Morunos means "Moorish" and they are certainly "more-ish." Use good-quality pork (a southern Spanish substitute for the Moors' lamb), preferably organic, in order to make tender, highly flavored kabobs. Ideally, cook them on a barbecue, but they taste fine when broiled in an oven.

FOR 4 TAPAS

3 tbsp. olive oil

2 tbsp. white wine vinegar

¼ tsp. ground cumin

¼ tsp. sweet paprika

¼ tsp. hot paprika

2 tbsp. chopped parsley

2 cloves of garlic, finely chopped

1 lb. 2 oz. lean pork, cut into 1-inch cubes

salt and pepper to taste

4 wooden or metal skewers

Prepare a marinade by mixing all the ingredients, except for the pork cubes, salt, and pepper.

Pour the marinade over the pork cubes and leave for 48 hours in the refrigerator.

Thread the pork onto the skewers and grill on a high heat for four to five minutes on each side, until all sides are brown. Sprinkle with salt and pepper and serve at once.

- ANCHOA
- BOLETUS CON JAMÓN
- QUESO DE CABRA
- PIQUILLO CON GAMBAS
- PIQUILLO CON SOLOMILLO

- ~~ERGON,~~ ALCACHOFAS Y HABITAS
- JAMÓN IBERICO, HABITAS Y SALMÓN
- CECINA DE MORUCHA

MICHIRONES A LA MURCIANA

FAVA BEAN, HAM, AND SAUSAGE STEW

This popular recipe originated in Murcia, Spain's smallest autonomous region, which lies between Valencia and Andalucía. It is similar to the spicy fava bean and pork stew from Bodega Montaña (see page 77), but the beef stock makes this a meatier dish.

FOR 6 TAPAS

1 lb. 2 oz. dried fava beans, soaked for 48 hours

¼ lb. chorizo or other spicy sausage, cut into ½-inch slices

¼ lb. serrano ham, thickly cut and diced

1 ham bone

2 dry red chili peppers, finely chopped

7 cups beef stock

salt to taste

Place all the ingredients, in the order in which they appear in the ingredients list, in a large saucepan. Pour in just enough stock to cover.

Cover the pan and place over a high heat. When the mixture comes to a boil, turn down the heat and cook slowly for one to two hours or until the beans are tender. Top up the stock from time to time, if necessary.

Remove the ham bone. Season with salt and pepper (adding salt before this stage would make the beans hard) and serve hot in individual earthenware dishes with chunks of French bread or a few breadsticks.

PULARDA RELLENA DE FRUTOS SECOS EN SALSA DE ZARZAMORA

CHICKEN LEGS WITH PRUNES AND NUTS IN BLACKBERRY SAUCE

Moorish influences sing in this luscious concoction of prunes, nuts, dried fruit, chicken, and sweet wine. Remember that you can substitute any dark dessert wine for the Málaga variety.

FOR 12 TAPAS

⅔ cup pine nuts

about ⅓ cup chopped walnuts

about ⅓ cup unsalted pistachio nuts, shelled and chopped

5 oz. pitted prunes, chopped

12 organic, boneless chicken legs

salt and pepper to taste

2 tbsp. olive oil

½ lb. garlic cloves

2 potatoes, cut into ⅛-inch slices

2 small onions, sliced into half-moons

1 cup sweet Málaga wine

FOR THE BLACKBERRY SAUCE

5 oz. fresh or frozen blackberries

½ cup granulated sugar

2 tbsp. balsamic vinegar

Mix the nuts and prunes together, then stuff the chicken legs with the mixture. Tie each leg together with kitchen string.

Place the stuffed legs on baking sheets, season, drizzle with olive oil, surround with garlic cloves, onions, and potatoes, and bake in an oven preheated to 400°F for 30 to 35 minutes, until the chicken is cooked.

To make the sauce, heat the berries and sugar with a few tablespoons of water, stirring to dissolve the sugar in the berry juices. Add the vinegar, bring to a boil, then cook until syrupy; it will thicken more as it cools. Set aside.

Gently warm the wine over a low heat. Transfer the chicken legs, garlic, and onions to a platter, pour on the wine, and flambé immediately by touching the edge of the platter with the flame of a match. Serve the chicken accompanied by the sauce.

PATATAS CORTIJERAS CON PICADILLO DE CHORIZO

COUNTRY-STYLE POTATOES WITH CHORIZO AND PEPPERS

This recipe exploits the abundant fresh local vegetables, with the chorizo and ham acting as little more than seasoning. It's a perfect, sustaining combination enveloped by lightly cooked egg.

FOR 4 TAPAS

14 oz. potatoes, peeled and thinly sliced

¼ cup butter

¼ cup olive oil for frying

4 oz. onion, thinly sliced

1 oz. red pepper, thinly sliced

1 oz. green pepper, thinly sliced

3 cloves of garlic, thinly sliced

1 oz. serrano ham or prosciutto,
    cut into thin strips

2 oz. chorizo or similar spicy sausage, cut into
    ½-inch slices and lightly fried

2 eggs

salt and pepper to taste

Fry the potatoes in the butter and two tablespoons of the oil over a very low heat for about 25 minutes, until tender. Remove, leaving the fat behind, and put them in a large bowl. Set aside.

In the same pan, sauté the onion and peppers, adding more oil if needed. When these are tender, add the garlic and cook until golden.

Add the vegetables to the potatoes, stir in the meats, and set aside.

Fry the eggs in a little oil until the white is firm. Add them to the vegetable and meat mixture and stir to break up the eggs. Combine all the ingredients, season, and tip onto a serving platter.

FRIED PORK LOIN AND HAM BALLS

Quite simply delicious, this is an excellent tapa for large numbers of people, as the meatballs can be prepared in advance and served cold. The zing of the lemon juice makes all the difference. Delicious with an accompaniment such as sliced pan-fried potatoes and poached onion.

FOR 6 TAPAS

8 oz. pork loin, cut into thin strips

juice of 1 lemon

4 oz. Iberian or serrano ham (or prosciutto)

salt and pepper to taste

2 tbsp. all-purpose flour

2 eggs, beaten

½ cup dried breadcrumbs

olive oil, for frying

Marinate the pork loin in the lemon juice for one hour.

Place a piece of ham on each pork strip, season, and roll up lengthwise to form cylinders.

Cut each cylinder into one-inch pieces, and shape these into balls.

Dip the balls in the flour, then the egg, then the breadcrumbs, and fry a few at a time in very hot oil, browning on all sides. Drain on paper towels and serve promptly.

LENTEJAS ESTOFADAS
LENTIL AND CHORIZO STEW

Well-blended, earthy flavors are the characteristics of this classic tapa, simply prepared according to Diego's tastes.

FOR 4 TAPAS

- - - - - - - - - - - -

8 oz. green or brown lentils, soaked overnight

about ⅓ cup virgin olive oil

1½ tsp. paprika

1 small green pepper, diced

1 small onion, diced

1 small, ripe tomato, peeled and diced

1 bay leaf

3 cloves of garlic

4 oz. chorizo or other spicy sausage, sliced

4 oz. blood sausage, sliced

1 small carrot, peeled and sliced

8 oz. potatoes, peeled and diced

Combine all the ingredients, except the potatoes, in a heavy saucepan. Cover with cold water and bring to a boil. Reduce the heat and simmer for about 20 minutes.

Add the potatoes and continue to simmer for about 10 more minutes, until the potatoes and lentils are tender. Serve hot in individual soup bowls or dishes.

SALTEADO DE HÍGADO DE COCHINILLO CON SETAS Y PIÑONES

SAUTÉED PORK LIVER WITH MUSHROOMS AND PINE NUTS

At the long-established José Maria restaurant in Segovia, this dish is prepared with liver from a recently slaughtered suckling pig. It has quite a strong flavor so, vary the quantity of mushrooms to balance the dish.

Sauté the pork liver in a little olive oil and set aside. Sauté the mushrooms and garlic in two tablespoons of olive oil until tender. Add the liver and cook until done.

Create a mound of the liver and mushrooms on a serving plate, splash with the vinegar, garnish with the pine nuts, and serve at once.

FOR 6 TAPAS

3 young pigs' livers, coarsely chopped

olive oil

3 oz. wild mushrooms, sliced

1 clove of garlic, minced

1 tbsp. white wine vinegar

2 tbsp. pine nuts

HABAS CONDIMENTADAS

SPICY FAVA BEAN AND PORK STEW

Typical of southern Spanish peasant food, this tapa contrasts the satisfying earthiness of pork and other meats with the mellow fava beans—a legume that is undergoing a revival.

FOR 6 TAPAS

1 lb. 2 oz. dried fava beans, soaked for 48 hours

1 oz. lomo ibérico (cured pork loin)

1 oz. cured beef

2 oz. chorizo or other spicy sausage

1 oz. smoked ham

1 small ham bone

¼ lb. chistorra or pork sausage

a handful (about 1 oz.) fresh mint leaves

6 bay leaves

1 tsp. cayenne pepper

7 cups chicken stock or water

4 tbsp. olive oil

about 2 tbsp. hot, smoked Spanish paprika (*pimentón de la Vera*)

salt and pepper to taste

Place all the ingredients (except the olive oil, paprika, and salt) in a large saucepan, in the order in which they appear in the ingredients list, then use just enough stock or water to cover the rest of the ingredients.

Heat the olive oil in a small frying pan, add the paprika, and stir until well blended. Pour this over the bean mixture, cover the pan, and place on a high heat. When the mixture comes to a boil, turn down the heat and cook slowly for one to two hours or until the beans are tender. Add extra stock from time to time, if necessary.

Remove the ham bone. Season the stew with salt and pepper (adding salt before this stage would make the beans hard), and serve hot in individual earthenware dishes.

MARISCOS Y PESCADOS

SEAFOOD

PAELLA DE BACALAO Y ESPINACAS

COD, SPINACH, AND TOMATO PAELLA

Of the myriad of forms of paella, this is one of the most delicious, with its distinctive flavor and dark color. You can replace the salt cod with fresh cod, but it is essential to use medium, round-grained rice. Aim for classic Calasparra rice, this absorbs masses of liquid therefore punches even more flavor than other varieties.

FOR 6 TAPAS

1 lb. 2 oz. fresh spinach, washed, stalks removed

4 tbsp. olive oil

6 oz. salt cod

2 tbsp. pine nuts

½ lb. tomatoes, chopped

2 cloves of garlic, crushed

2 tsp. paprika

1 dried chili pepper, chopped

½ lb. Calasparra rice

2¼ cups vegetable stock

½ tsp. saffron threads, infused in 2 tbsp. of boiling water for 15 minutes

salt to taste

lemon wedges to serve

Soak the salt cod in water for 48 hours, changing the water a couple of times a day. Rinse. Cut the flesh into strips, leaving any bones and the skin behind.

In a covered saucepan, using only the water left on the leaves after washing, cook the spinach over a medium heat for four minutes. Squeeze out the excess water and chop.

Heat the oil in a large frying pan. When very hot, add the cod, spinach, pine nuts, tomatoes, garlic, paprika, and dried chili. Lower the heat and cook, stirring constantly, for six minutes.

Add the rice and continue to cook, stirring constantly, for two minutes. Add the stock and saffron. Season with salt and simmer for about 15 minutes or until the stock has been absorbed and the rice is just tender.

Remove from the heat, cover with a dishcloth, put the lid on, and allow to stand for five minutes. Garnish with lemon wedges and serve at once.

PINTXO DE SALMON AHUMADO CON BOQUERONES Y PIMIENTOS

SMOKED SALMON, ANCHOVY, AND RED PEPPER TOASTS

Pintxo **get their name from the toothpick, or literally "spike", that traditionally holds these delicious morsels together.**

FOR 4 TAPAS

4 fresh anchovies, marinated in vinegar (*boquerones*)

¼ lb. smoked salmon, cut into 4 slices and rolled into cylindrical shapes

1 red piquillo pepper (or ½ red bell pepper), cut into 4 equal parts

4 slices whole-wheat bread, toasted

FOR THE VINAIGRETTE

1 spring onion, finely chopped

2 red piquillo peppers or 1 red bell pepper, deseeded and finely chopped

1 hard-boiled egg, finely chopped

½ green pepper, deseeded and finely chopped

7 oz. extra-virgin olive oil

5 tbsp. white wine vinegar

To make the vinaigrette, combine the ingredients and mix well. Set aside.

To prepare the pintxo, place the anchovies skin-side down and put a roll of salmon in the center of each. Fold in half and top with a piece of piquillo pepper.

Place each anchovy roll on top of a slice of whole-wheat toast and drizzle generously with vinaigrette.

BACALAO AHUMADO Y VINAGRETA DE TOMATE CON ACEITE DE ACEITUNA NEGRA

SMOKED COD, TOMATO, AND BLACK-OLIVE OIL TOASTS

There is a beguiling balance between the slightly sharp smoked cod and the earthy black-olive oil in this recipe. A spoonful of French tapenade (olive paste) could easily be substituted for the olives in the oil. However, don't skip the whole-wheat bread—it's crucial to the balance of the dish.

FOR 8 TAPAS

8 slices whole-wheat bread, toasted

½ lb. raw smoked cod, thinly sliced

2 tbsp. chopped chives or parsley

FOR THE VINAIGRETTE

1 large, ripe tomato, peeled, pulp removed, and finely chopped

5 tbsp. extra-virgin olive oil

1½ tbsp. white wine vinegar

salt and pepper to taste

FOR THE BLACK-OLIVE OIL

2 oz. pitted black olives, finely chopped

½ cup extra-virgin olive oil

Prepare the vinaigrette by mixing the tomato with the olive oil, white wine vinegar, and seasoning.

Prepare the black-olive oil by adding the chopped olives to the olive oil and blending together well.

Just before serving, place eight toasts on a serving plate and moisten each with about one teaspoon of black-olive oil.

Put a slice of smoked cod on top of each toast and dress with a heaping tablespoon of vinaigrette and a little more black-olive oil. Garnish with chives or parsley.

ROLLITO DE CALABACÍN CON GAMBA Y BACON

FRIED ZUCCHINI, SHRIMP, AND BACON BUNDLES

This *pintxo* is a little tricky to prepare, but once you have mastered the technique you will use it again and again.

Cut the zucchini in half lengthwise, then cut four half-inch slices, again lengthwise, from one of the halves.

On each slice, lay one strip of bacon and place one shrimp, then season with salt and pepper.

Roll up the zucchini, ensuring that the shrimp stays in the center, and secure with a toothpick.

Carefully dip the bundle in the egg, then the flour. Heat about one inch of olive oil in a frying pan and cook the rolls until golden. Drain on a paper towel.

Serve immediately on a sesame-seed cracker.

FOR 4 TAPAS

1 large zucchini

4 strips of lean bacon

4 jumbo shrimp, cooked and peeled

salt and pepper to taste

1 beaten egg, for coating

all-purpose flour, for coating

olive oil, for frying

4 sesame-seed crackers

ALMEJAS CON JAMÓN
CLAMS AND HAM IN CHILI SAUCE

The classic Catalan combination of sea and mountain ingredients features in this Cal Pep favorite. It is a simple but highly flavored dish that can easily be expanded to become a main course. Use mussels if you can't find clams.

In a large frying pan, sauté the clams, ham, and chili pepper in hot oil until the clams begin to open. Discard any clams that have not opened by the time the dish is cooked.

Add the garlic, parsley, wine, salt, and pepper, and continue to cook for about two minutes. Spoon out into wide, shallow bowls, pour on the sauce, and serve immediately.

FOR 4 TAPAS

2 tbsp. olive oil, to sauté

10½ oz. fresh clams, thoroughly cleaned (discard any that are not closed)

2 oz. ham, cut in thin strips

1 medium red chili pepper, deseeded and finely chopped

2 cloves of garlic, minced

2 tbsp. finely chopped Italian parsley

2 tbsp. white wine

salt and pepper to taste

ANCHOA CON HUEVOS DE TRUCHA
ANCHOVY AND TROUT CAVIAR TOASTS

This classic recipe is a favorite among customers at Bar Txepetxa in San Sebastian and it is simple to make.

FOR 4 TAPAS

8 anchovy fillets, marinated in vinegar
4 slices of French bread, freshly toasted
4 tsp. trout eggs

For each *pintxo*, lay two anchovy fillets on a slice of freshly toasted French bread.

Place one teaspoon of trout eggs in a line down the middle of each toast. Serve immediately.

ANCHOA SALMÓN AHUMADO
ANCHOVY AND SMOKED SALMON TOASTS

A simple, subtle, yet extravagant-tasting *pintxo*. To ensure complete success, use the best smoked salmon you can find.

FOR 4 TAPAS

8 anchovy fillets, marinated in vinegar
4 slices of French bread, freshly toasted
2 slices smoked salmon, cut into strips

For each *pintxo*, lay two anchovy fillets on a slice of freshly toasted French bread.

Top each toast with a little mound of smoked salmon strips. Serve immediately.

ANCHOA JARDINERA

ANCHOVY AND VEGETABLE TOASTS

This deliciously fresh _pintxo_ takes place of honor on a plate of mixed anchovy toasts, adding a splash of color and a crisp texture.

Marinate the vegetables in the sunflower oil for half an hour to keep them from drying out and to leave them glistening.

For each _pintxo_, lay two anchovy fillets on a slice of freshly toasted French bread. Spoon some of themarinated vegetables on top of the anchovies. Serve immediately.

FOR 4 TAPAS

1 small green pepper, finely chopped

1 small red pepper, finely chopped

1 small onion, finely chopped

2 cloves of garlic, finely chopped

1 chili pepper, halved, deseeded, and finely chopped

a small bunch of fresh parsley, finely chopped

3 tbsp. sunflower oil

8 anchovy fillets, marinated in vinegar

4 slices of French bread, freshly toasted

LOMOS DE ANCHOA CON CREMA DE CENTOLLA

ANCHOVY AND CRAB TOASTS

A real taste of the sea! If you prefer a meatier flavor, add a slice of finely chopped ham to the crab mixture.

Mix together the crab, lettuce, and egg. Stir in the mayonnaise and lemon juice.

For each _pintxo_, lay two anchovy fillets on a slice of freshly toasted French bread, then cover with the crab mixture. Serve immediately.

FOR 4 TAPAS

meat of 1 cooked crab, finely chopped

2 lettuce leaves, finely shredded

1 hard-boiled egg, chopped

2 tbsp. mayonnaise

2 tsp. lemon juice

8 anchovy fillets marinated in vinegar

4 slices of French bread, freshly toasted

LOMOS DE ANCHOA CON PÂTÉ DE OLIVAS

ANCHOVY, TAPENADE, AND ONION TOASTS

An intense-tasting *pintxo*—the one none of your guests will be able to forget! Delicious as an appetizer.

FOR 4 TAPAS

1 small onion, finely chopped

2 tbsp. lemon juice

8 anchovy fillets, marinated in vinegar

4 slices of French bread, freshly toasted

3 tbsp. tapenade (olive paste)

Marinate the onion in lemon juice for at least two hours prior to serving the tapas.

For each *pintxo*, put two anchovy fillets on a slice of freshly toasted French bread, cover with two teaspoons of tapenade, then sprinkle with the chopped onion. Serve immediately.

SUQUET DE PESCADO
CATALAN FISH STEW

This Catalan classic goes well beyond the quantity boundaries of tapas, so it can move up your menu to slot in as a first or second course. It is excellent served with purées of eggplant and potatoes, which are both good for soaking up the ambrosial fish juices.

FOR 4 TAPAS

olive oil

2 cloves of garlic, crushed

2 tbsp. chopped fresh parsley

2 tomatoes, peeled, deseeded, and chopped

4¼ cups fish stock

4 medium-sized new potatoes, peeled and diced

½ tsp. sweet Spanish paprika

salt and pepper to taste

4 (6-oz.) fish fillets, such as cod

In a little olive oil, sauté the garlic in a large frying pan until soft but not browned. Add the parsley and tomatoes and cook over a low heat, stirring, until the mixture thickens.

Add the fish stock, potatoes, and paprika to the tomatoes and cook for about 10 minutes or until the potatoes are tender. Season the dish with salt and pepper to taste.

While the stew is cooking, broil the fish fillets, skin-side down, until golden.

Serve the fish stew at once in bowls, with the fillets on the side.

TXALUPA

MUSHROOM, SHRIMP, AND CHEESE TARTLETS

Typically subtle in flavor, this *pintxo* also looks terrific. Be sure to serve this with a refreshing white wine.

FOR 8 TAPAS

¼ lb. mushrooms, chopped

2 cloves of garlic, finely minced

2 tbsp. butter

salt to taste

½ cup sparkling white wine

½ cup heavy cream

10 cooked jumbo shrimp, peeled and chopped

¼ lb. mature cheddar cheese, grated

FOR THE 8 TARTLET CASES

½ cup all-purpose flour

a pinch of salt

3 tbsp. butter, softened

1 egg yolk

a little cold water

Make the pastry. Prepare and cook the pastry cases according to steps one and two in the recipe on page 93, omitting the pastry lids.

To make the filling, sauté the mushrooms and garlic in butter over a low heat for 20 minutes. Sprinkle with salt to taste, add the white wine, bring to a boil, and cook until there is barely any liquid left. Add the cream and shrimp and continue to cook for three minutes, stirring occasionally. Remove from the heat.

Remove the pastry shells from their pans. Fill with the shrimp mixture and top with grated cheese. Grill for two minutes or until the cheese is golden. Serve immediately.

HOJALDRE RELLENO
BLUE CHEESE AND ANCHOVY TARTLETS

Hidden between the pastry shells lies a rich, flavorful filling, so be sure to serve this *pintxo* with a refreshing white wine. Txakoli, the Basque favorite, is ideal, but in its absence, look for a light, dry, sparkling white.

FOR 8 TAPAS

2 oz. Stilton or other soft blue cheese, crumbled

1 cup heavy cream, whipped

4 anchovy fillets in oil, drained and halved

FOR THE 8 TARTLET CASES

1 cup all-purpose flour

½ tsp. salt

½ cup butter, softened

2 egg yolks

a little cold water

extra flour, for rolling out

To make the pastry, put the flour, salt, and butter in a food processor and process with the pastry blade until the mixture resembles fine breadcrumbs. Add the egg yolks, mixed with a bit of water, a little at a time, continuing to blend. Add just enough to make the pastry come together in a ball—don't make it wet. Wrap the pastry in plastic wrap and refrigerate for half an hour.

Roll out the pastry on a floured surface and cut it to fit eight small tart pans. Also cut out some lids for each tartlet. Prick the bottoms of the tartlets and chill for 20 minutes. Fill the tartlets with a few dried beans so that they can "bake blind." Put the lids on a baking sheet and cook both cases and lids in a preheated oven at 400°F for about 15 minutes or until pale gold. Cool in the pans.

For the filling, blend the cheese and whipped cream with a wooden spoon until smooth. Set aside.

Remove the tartlet shells from their pans and place half an anchovy on the bottom of each. Cover with the cheese and cream mixture and top with a pastry lid.

Place the pastries on a baking sheet and heat in a 425°F oven for one minute. Remove and serve.

QUESO, ANCHOA, PIMIENTO Y PUERRO SOBRE HOJALDRE

RED PEPPER, LEEK, ANCHOVY, AND CREAM CHEESE TARTS

This two-bite tapa is quick to make as well as to consume, yet the pastry case makes it satisfyingly filling. The quantity of anchovy or red pepper can be increased according to your taste.

FOR 4 TAPAS

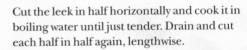

1 leek, white portion only

4 anchovy fillets, drained of oil

½ small red pepper, roasted, peeled, and cut into 4 equal strips

4 (4-inch) squares of puff pastry, cooked

4 oz. cream cheese

Cut the leek in half horizontally and cook it in boiling water until just tender. Drain and cut each half in half again, lengthwise.

Place one anchovy and one small strip of red pepper on each puff pastry square, then spread carefully with an ounce of cream cheese and top with a piece of leek.

Place under a broiler for just long enough to heat through (about three to four minutes) and serve immediately.

SARDINES MARINATED IN CHILI, GARLIC, AND BAY LEAVES

Simple, grilled sardines are ubiquitous throughout Spain, but here, the marinade transforms them into an aromatic sensation. While this tapa is explicitly garlicky, the slight bitterness of the bay leaves gives it a cutting edge. Just as with many dishes, it tastes even better a day later.

FOR 6 TAPAS

12 medium, fresh sardines, scaled and gutted

all-purpose flour, for coating

½ cup olive oil

black pepper to taste

1 dry red chili pepper, minced

12 cloves of garlic

1 tbsp. sweet paprika

3 bay leaves

½ cup white wine vinegar

½ cup dry white wine

½ cup water

salt to taste

At least 2½ hours before serving, coat the sardines lightly with flour on both sides and quickly fry in hot oil to brown each side. Place in a shallow earthenware dish.

Strain the oil that was used to fry the sardines and, when cool, return it to the frying pan and add the pepper, chili pepper, and garlic cloves. Fry gently until the garlic is golden.

Remove from the heat and add the paprika, bay leaves, vinegar, wine, water, and salt. Bring to a boil for one minute.

Pour the hot liquid over the sardines and leave to marinate at room temperature for at least two hours.

These sardines can be served hot, cold, or at room temperature.

MEJILLONES EN SALSA PICANTE

MUSSELS IN SPICY SAUCE

It is essential to broil this dish just before you serve it; that way, it tastes fresh and hot. Find mussels that are as plump, juicy, and fresh as possible and choose cheese with a sharp, tangy flavor, such as a mature cheddar.

FOR 4 TAPAS

4 bay leaves

salt and pepper to taste

2 lb. 4 oz. mussels, scrubbed, discarding any that do not close

¼ cup olive oil

1 large onion, chopped

6 cloves of garlic, finely chopped

½ red chili pepper, deseeded and finely chopped

1 tsp. all-purpose flour

1½ tsp. hot, smoked Spanish paprika (pimentón de la Vera)

½ lb. Cebreiro cheese, or similar sharp cheese that melts well, grated

In a deep, heavy pan, bring about ½ cup of water, two bay leaves, and a pinch of salt to a boil. Add the mussels, cover, and cook for about four to five minutes, until the shells open.

Remove the mussels from the pan, discarding any that haven't opened. Remove one shell from each cooked mussel and discard. Place the mussels in their half-shells in a shallow, ovenproof dish, pour the cooking liquid over them, and set aside.

Heat the oil in a large frying pan. Add the onion, garlic, chili, and two remaining bay leaves. Sauté gently over a low heat until the onion turns golden.

Stir in the flour and paprika and cook for one minute, stirring constantly.

Remove from the heat and slowly add the mussel cooking liquid, stirring it in throughly. Put the pan back on the heat and cook until the sauce thickens. Remove from the heat and mix in a blender to achieve a smooth sauce.

Return the sauce to the pan. Add the mussels and cook for three to four minutes. Arrange the mussels and sauce in a heatproof serving bowl, sprinkle with grated cheese, and broil gently, until the cheese has melted. Serve this dish immediately.

BONITO EN SASHIMI MARINADO

MARINATED TUNA CUBES

Carlos Abellan serves this tapa in a porcelain dish specially designed for such cubes, but the food's so stylish it would look good on almost anything. Make sure the tuna is ultrafresh, as this is the heart of the dish. For an even more intense flavor, lightly sprinkle either some powdered ginger or grated fresh ginger over the cubes.

Prepare the marinade by mixing the soy sauce and sunflower oil together. Add the tuna and leave it to marinate for at least 12 hours.

Thread the tuna cubes onto thin skewers. Sprinkle each cube with a few sesame seeds and drizzle with a little soy oil. Serve promptly.

FOR 4 TAPAS

¼ cup soy sauce

¼ cup sunflower oil

5½ oz. fresh tuna, cut into 1¼-inch cubes

2 tbsp. sesame seeds

soy oil

VENTRESCA DE ATÚN CONFITADA CON ARROZ A LA CRÈME DE GINGEMBRE

ROASTED TUNA SERVED WITH GINGERED RICE

The tender, fresh fish and sweet red onion are perfectly complemented by the delicate ginger flavor of the rice. It is essential to respect the baking time in order to preserve the flaky texture and color of the tuna. This dish looks wonderful on a large platter or served in small, flat bowls. If the ingredients are multiplied, it works equally well as a main course.

FOR 4 TAPAS

1 tbsp. butter

½ tsp. finely chopped fresh ginger

about ⅓ cup long-grain rice

3 tbsp. heavy cream

2 tbsp. finely chopped parsley, plus 1 tbsp. for garnish

salt and white pepper to taste

½-lb. belly of tuna fish, skinned and filleted

2 tbsp. finely chopped red onion

extra-virgin olive oil, for drizzling

Melt the butter in a saucepan and sauté the ginger for about a minute. Add the rice, stir it around in the butter and ginger, and add ½ cup of water. Bring to a boil, turn down the heat, cover, and cook for about 15 minutes. The rice should be tender but not completely soft, and the water should have evaporated. Stir in the cream, parsley, salt, and pepper. Keep warm.

Preheat the oven to 325°F. Cut the tuna into four equal parts, then arrange in a single layer in a lightly oiled ovenproof dish. Cover tightly with aluminum foil and place in the oven. Cook for five minutes.

Remove from the oven, salt lightly, and transfer to a serving plate. Arrange the pieces in a ring, leaving a space in the center for the rice. Sprinkle each piece of tuna with chopped onion and parsley. Drizzle with extra-virgin olive oil.

Spoon the creamy gingered rice into the center of the plate and serve immediately.

ANCHOA CON QUESO

ANCHOVY AND SHEEP CHEESE ON TOAST

A wonderfully salty tapa. The sheep cheese and anchovy combine to create a powerful flavor.

Lightly toast the slices of French bread on each side.

Place one slice of sheep cheese on each piece of toast, then top with an anchovy fillet.

FOR 4 TAPAS

4 slices of French bread
4 slices of sheep cheese
4 anchovy fillets

LOMO IBÉRICO DE BELLOTA, KAVIAR O SALMÓN AHUMADO

ORGANIC CURED BEEF, CAVIAR, OR SMOKED SALMON ON TOAST

These *pintxos* from José Luis are more ideas than recipes, but they make luxuriously simple snacks and look great on a plate together topped with mayonnaise.

Lightly toast the slices of French bread on each side until golden.

Place slices of the best-quality cured beef on four pieces of toast, a heaping spoonful of caviar on the next four, and a slice of smoked salmon on each of the remaining pieces.

FOR 12 TAPAS

12 slices of French bread
4 slices cured beef
¼ lb. caviar
4 slices of smoked salmon

TARTAR DE AHUMADOS
SMOKED FISH TARTAR

A delicious combination of three smoked fish, this is another salty tapa that makes a terrific appetizer. The onion and capers add a piquancy that will really set your mouth watering.

Lightly toast the French bread on each side.

Mix the smoked anchovies, salmon, and trout together. Add the chopped onion and capers and blend well. Mix in the mayonnaise.

Heap a large spoonful of the paste onto each toast, and serve.

FOR 4 TAPAS

4 slices of French bread

2 oz. smoked anchovies, finely chopped

2 oz. smoked salmon, finely chopped

2 oz. smoked trout, finely chopped

2 tsp. diced onion

2 tsp. diced capers

3 oz. mayonnaise

SARDE EN SAOR

MARINATED SARDINES WITH ONIONS IN SHERRY

Michele Gallana of Valencía learned this traditional Venetian sailor's way of marinating sardines from his grandmother. To give it a Valencian touch, mix in a handful of pine nuts and raisins just before serving.

Coat the sardines with flour and fry them in a thin layer of hot oil until they are delicately browned on both sides. Drain on paper towels.

In a separate pan, slowly fry the onions in oil until they are golden. Remove from the heat, add the vinegar and seasoning, and stir well.

Alternate layers of sardines and onions in a deep dish, beginning with sardines and ending with the onions. Cool and refrigerate for at least two hours.

To serve, spoon generous portions onto individual plates.

FOR 6 TAPAS

1 lb. 2 oz. small, fresh sardines, gutted and scaled

all-purpose flour for coating

olive oil, for frying

4 onions, finely chopped

½ cup white wine vinegar

salt and pepper to taste

MEJILLONES À LA MARINERA
FISHERMEN'S MUSSELS

Choose large, plump mussels to complement the generous tomato sauce with its aromatic echoes of the Mediterranean.

FOR 6 TAPAS

1 lb. 10 oz. fresh mussels, scrubbed, any open ones discarded

about ⅓ cup dry white wine

1 bay leaf

2 tbsp. olive oil

1 large onion, finely chopped

1 red pepper, finely chopped

1 green pepper, finely chopped

2 cloves of garlic, finely chopped

2 ripe tomatoes, finely chopped

a pinch of cayenne pepper

white pepper to taste

Place the mussels in a large pot with the wine and bay leaf, and cook, covered, over a high heat for a few minutes, shaking occasionally, until all the shells have opened (discard any that do not). Transfer the mussels to a serving platter and keep them warm. Reserve the cooking liquid.

Heat the olive oil in a saucepan. Sauté the onion, peppers, and garlic until tender. Add the tomatoes and cayenne pepper and cook for about 15 minutes, until the mixture is thick. Stir in a little of the cooking liquid and season with white pepper.

Pour the sauce over the mussels and serve at once.

ESCALIBADA CON CABALLA EN ESCABECHE
MARINATED MACKEREL WITH ROASTED VEGETABLES

Escalibada is an eastern Spanish classic that makes full use of the abundant fresh vegetables grown locally. The name comes from the Catalan word for "charred," and ideally the vegetables should be cooked over a barbecue to get a really full, smoky flavor. *Escalibada* can be served with any kind of preserved or marinated fish, though mackerel works perfectly.

FOR 6 TAPAS

1 eggplant, halved lengthwise

1 zucchini, halved lengthwise

1 onion, peeled and quartered

1 red pepper, halved and deseeded

1 fennel bulb, trimmed, quartered, and heart removed

olive oil, for roasting

ground rock salt to taste

½ cup dry white wine

1 cup olive oil

4 mackerel fillets

6 cloves

4 cloves of garlic, unpeeled

4 bay leaves

Place the vegetables (except for the garlic) cut-side down on a baking sheet, brush with olive oil, season with rock salt, and roast at 400°F for 35 minutes. Remove from the oven and set aside.

For the marinade, whisk together the wine and olive oil. Put the mackerel fillets in a wide saucepan and pour over just enough marinade to cover them. Add the cloves, garlic, and bay leaves, cover, and simmer for 15 minutes.

Peel the skin from the roast pepper halves and cut the stem off the eggplant halves. Slice the vegetables thinly and arrange in the center of a plate. Place the mackerel fillets on top of the vegetables and garnish the rim of the plate with the bay leaves and garlic cloves. This tapa can be served warm or cool, but not refrigerated.

FIDEOS A LA MARINERA
SEAFOOD PASTA

Although tricky to prepare, this tapa looks and tastes so terrific that you may want to increase the quantities to make it into a main dish.

FOR 6 TAPAS

----

1 medium onion, diced

2 medium green peppers, diced

2 tomatoes, diced

2 cloves of garlic, minced

olive oil, for frying

about ⅓ cup white wine

4½ cups water

¼ tsp. saffron threads, infused in boiling water

½ lb. clams, well-scrubbed; discard any that will not close

6 oz. cuttlefish, cleaned and cut into small strips

6 oz. shrimp, peeled

4 oz. hake or cod, filleted and cut into small pieces

salt and pepper to taste

8 oz. short lengths of spaghetti or a pasta shape such as *tubetti lunghi*

chopped parsley to garnish

In a casserole or heavy-bottomed sauté pan, fry the onion, peppers, tomatoes, and garlic in the olive oil until soft.

Add the white wine and cook for about 10 minutes to reduce the liquid.

Add the water and saffron liquid and cook over a high heat for 15 minutes.

Add the clams, cuttlefish, shrimp, hake, seasoning, and pasta noodles and continue to cook over a low heat for about 10 minutes, until the fish and pasta are tender and the liquid has been absorbed. Discard any clams that have not opened. Serve in individual earthenware dishes, decorated with parsley.

PUDIN DE ESPINACAS

SPINACH AND SHRIMP LOAF

This cold, mousse-like tapa is ideal for hot weather, when appetites are not too big. This tapa makes the perfect accompaniment for a glass of beer or sangría in the summer.

FOR 4 TAPAS

14 oz. spinach, washed and destalked

1 medium onion, finely chopped

2 medium tomatoes, finely chopped

2 tbsp. olive oil

¼ lb. raw shrimp, peeled

salt and pepper to taste

½ cup milk

½ cup heavy cream

4 eggs

In a covered saucepan, cook the spinach, using only the water that clings to the leaves after washing, over a medium heat for about four minutes. Drain, and wring out the excess water by pressing the cooked leaves between two dinner plates; the spinach must be very dry. Set aside.

Sauté the onion and tomatoes in the olive oil until tender. Turn up the heat and allow some of the liquid to evaporate. Add the spinach and shrimp, season, and stir. Cook over a low heat for three to four minutes, then cool.

Put the shrimp and spinach mixture into a blender and add the milk, cream, and eggs. Blend until smooth and creamy. Season to taste.

Pour into a lightly oiled loaf pan. Place the loaf pan into a roasting pan filled with two to three inches of water. Bake at 350°F for about 45 minutes, until firm (a skewer inserted into the center should come out clean). Cool, then refrigerate for at least two hours.

To serve, turn out of the pan and cut into slices of the desired thickness. Serve with a seasonal salad of your choice.

PURRUSALDA
POTATO AND COD STEW

The classic marriage of cod and potatoes has been developed into a hearty, appetizing tapa, lifted by tomatoes and olive oil.

FOR 4 TAPAS

8 oz. salt cod

4 leeks, cleaned and coarsely chopped

4 tbsp. olive oil

2 lb. 4 oz. potatoes, peeled and diced

11 cups fish stock

3 ripe tomatoes, chopped

salt and pepper to taste

Soak the salt cod in water for 48 hours, changing the water twice a day. Rinse. Flake the flesh, leaving any bones and the skin behind.

In a large saucepan or stockpot, sauté the leeks in the oil until tender. Add the potatoes, then sauté over a very low heat for 15 more minutes.

Add the fish stock and tomatoes, bring to a boil, and simmer for 20 minutes.

Add the flaked salt cod and simmer for 10 minutes. Season to taste and serve hot in individual soup bowls.

PUDIN DE ESPÁRRAGOS VERDES Y GAMBAS

ASPARAGUS AND SHRIMP TARTS

The Spanish word *pudin*, an aborted version of the English "pudding," is used to describe a savory tapa that resembles a French mousse. This version has a pleasingly rough texture and undemanding flavors.

FOR 4 TAPAS

½ medium onion, finely chopped

olive oil

4 oz. shrimp, peeled and chopped

4 oz. green asparagus, preferably wild, cut into small pieces

¼ cup dry sherry

1 cup whipping cream

3 eggs, beaten

salt and white pepper to taste

mayonnaise, to serve

A day before serving, sauté the onion in a little olive oil until soft. Add the shrimp, asparagus, and sherry, and cook over a low heat until the liquid has almost disappeared.

Add the cream, eggs, and a little salt and pepper, and mix well.

Pour into lightly oiled, individual tart pans. Set these into a roasting or cake pan filled with about a half-inch of water and bake in a 350°F oven for 35 minutes. Remove from the oven, cool, and then refrigerate for 12 hours.

Just before serving, turn out the tarts, place on individual plates, and top each with a spoonful of mayonnaise.

ENSALADA DE BACALAO CON
SALT COD AND ORANGE SALAD

This ultrasimple tapa offers a refreshing combination of flavors, but it is essential to use good-quality salt cod and luscious oranges. If you have individual molds, so much the better, as cutting slices of this dish tends to make it crumble.

FOR 4 TAPAS

1 lb. 12 oz. salt cod

11 oz. juicy orange segments, skin and seeds removed, diced

2 tbsp. chives, snipped

4 black olives

extra-virgin olive oil to taste

Soak the salt cod in water for 48 hours, changing the water twice a day. Remove the flesh and flake, discarding the skin and bones.

Mix the orange flesh with the chives, then divide the mixture into individual molds. Top with the flaked salt cod and compress well.

Refrigerate for at least one hour before turning upside down and sliding out onto plates to serve.

Decorate with a black olive and drizzle with olive oil.

PIMIENTOS DEL PIQUILLO RELLENOS

DEEP-FRIED RED PIQUILLO PEPPERS WITH TUNA STUFFING

Although piquillo peppers are grown in Navarra and Rioja, they are in demand throughout the country for their concentrated juiciness and sweetness. If you can't find fresh ones, use the canned variety.

FOR 4 TAPAS

8 whole red piquillo peppers, fresh or canned, or 4 red bell peppers

2 tbsp. butter

1 tbsp sunflower oil

about 2 tbsp. all-purpose flour

a pinch of cornstarch

1¼ cups milk

salt and pepper to taste

freshly grated nutmeg to taste

6 oz. canned tuna in oil, drained and flaked

1 beaten egg, for coating

all-purpose flour, for coating

olive or sunflower oil, for frying

If using fresh peppers, halve and deseed them, then broil until blistered and black in places. Leave them to cool, then peel off the skin.

To prepare the stuffing, make a white sauce by melting the butter in a pan with the sunflower oil. Add the flour and cornstarch, stirring constantly until the flours and fats come together and make a roux. Cook until the roux is pale gold, then remove from the heat. Add the milk, a little at a time, stirring well after each addition. Put the pan back on the heat and bring to a boil, stirring constantly to make a smooth sauce. Cook over a low heat, stirring from time to time, for five minutes.

Take the sauce off the heat and season well with salt, pepper, and nutmeg. Add the tuna and mix thoroughly, then allow to cool. Refrigerate for 12 hours.

About half an hour before serving, fill the peppers with the tuna mixture, being careful not to tear them. Fold over the filling. Dip the stuffed peppers in the egg, then in the flour and then carefully lower them into the hot oil with the slotted spoon. Fry in about four inches of hot oil until lightly browned on all sides. Drain on paper towels and serve immediately.

CALAMARES PICA-PICA

SQUID IN TOMATO, GARLIC, AND RED WINE SAUCE

Easy to make yet oozing with flavor, this Mallorcan tapa is a real hit in Valencia. Make sure the squid you use is small and tender.

FOR 4 TAPAS

½ cup olive oil

1 lb. 2 oz. squid, cleaned and cut into 2-inch pieces

1 onion, coarsely chopped

½ lb. tomatoes, coarsely chopped

2 cloves of garlic, crushed

1 red pepper, coarsely chopped

1 bay leaf

1 cup red wine

½ cup fish stock

chives to garnish

Heat the olive oil in a large saucepan. Add the squid and stir-fry for one minute. Add the onion and tomatoes and fry for five minutes.

Add the garlic, pepper, bay leaf, red wine, and stock. Stir, then simmer for 20 minutes. Serve hot in earthenware dishes, with a chive garnish and crusty bread.

CHEFS

Carles Abellán, Barcelona
With his elegant restaurant and tapas bar, Comerç24, Carles flung open the doors of fame. Then followed funky Tapaç24, then El Velódromo. Ferran Adrià being a past mentor, the food is fun, imaginative, yet rooted in Catalunya.
— Catalan fish stew 91
— Marinated tuna cubes 100

Bar Pinotxo, Barcelona
The Bayen family, commanded by bow-tied Juanito, runs the renowned little Bar Pinotxo inside the thronging Boquería market. Le tout Barcelona has sat on a stool here to sample their flavorful, freshly cooked Catalan tapas.
— Chickpeas with blood sausage in garlic and parsley 47
— Sardines marinated in chilli, garlic, and bay leaves 97

Enrique Becerra & Diego Ruiz, Seville
Backed by five generations in the restaurant business, Enrique Becerra's unrivalled knowledge of Sevillian food has put classics such as these on the menu of his acclaimed restaurant.
— Asparagus and shrimp tarts 115
— Lentil and chorizo stew 74
— Minted lamb meatballs 59

Luis Benavente, Madrid
Luis ran Bocaito, a charmingly old-fashioned bar-restaurant in central Madrid, until a few years ago. Some of his original tapas just never went away.
— Young garlic, fava bean, and ham omelette 35

Patxi Bergara & Blanca Ameztoy, San Sebastián
Bar Bergara, steered by this industrious husband-and-wife team, is an institution in the Gros district, making high quality, award-winning pintxos.
— Blue cheese and anchovy tartlets 93
— Mushroom, shrimp & cheese tartlets 92

Bodegas Campos, Córdoba
A series of chefs at the illustrious Bodegas Campos, a spectacular, rambling hacienda open since 1908, follow house tapas recipes that incorporate the best of Andalucian produce.
— Country-style potatoes with chorizo and peppers 70
— Fried pork loin and ham balls 73
— Fritata of garden vegetables 21

Rosas María Borja & Isabel Capote Domínguez, Seville
Borja and Domínguez, two brilliant, creative chefs , launched these tapas at Seville's La Eslava.
— Honey-baked chicken thighs 43
— Potato and cod stew 114
— Spinach shrimp loaf 112

Joaquín Campos, Madrid
Dynamic Joaquin has now jumped ship to live in Shanghai, taking tapas to the Chinese. He devised these dishes for a tapas bar in Madrid, although he originates from Malaga.
— Roasted tuna served with gingered rice 101
— Fried goat cheese with honey 36
— Iberian ham and fava bean salad 44

Michele Gallana, Valencia
When he ran the trailblazing Santa Companya wine bar, Michele, who hails from Venice in Italy, infused new gastronomic ideas into Valencia's offerings.
— Cheese and quince 39
— Marinated sardines with onions in sherry 105
— Spicy steak tartare 62

Emiliano García Domene, Valencia
Emiliano has owned the illustrious Bodega Montaña in Valencia's old fishing quarter for over 20 years, introducing wines from all over the world to accompany ambrosial tapas.

— Artichoke hearts with black-olive oil 12
— Deep-fried red piquillo peppers with tuna stuffing 119
— Spicy broad bean and pork stew 77

Lola Gracía Burgos & Emiliano Sánchez Pincón, Seville
Lola, wife of the owner of Bar Giralda, together with chef Emiliano, devise recipes for their constantly changing menu.
— Potatoes of great importance 20

Paco Guzmán, Barcelona
Guzmán, the impassioned chef-owner of fashionable restaurants Santa María and Santa, conjures up delectable fusion dishes derived from his experience working in France and Asia.
— Duck liver with sweet pears and Szechuan pepper 48
— Pumpkin, chestnut, feta cheese, and pomegranate salad 14

Josep Manubens, Barcelona
The Cal Pep bar is a Barcelona legend, prompting snaking queues of eager customers from all over the world. The reason for this is the astute yet creative tapas created by chef-owner Josep ('Pep'), all of which are cooked and served at the packed bar with fantastic aplomb.
— Clams and ham in chili sauce 86
— Tricky tortilla 29

Mari-Carmen Manuel & Josecho Marañón, San Sebastián
In the web of highly competitive pintxo bars in San Sebastián old town, right by the harbor, the Marañón family's Bar Txepetxa monopolizes the anchovy market.
— Anchovy and crab toasts 89
— Anchovy and smoked salmon toasts 88
— Anchovy and trout caviar toasts 88
— Anchovy and vegetable toasts 89
— Anchovy, tapenade, & onion toasts 90

Carlos Martinez & Meay Espinosa, Logroño

The capital of the Rioja wine region boasts an unrivalled concentration of bars in just one street, Calle Laurel. Casa Pali is one of these and serves simple tapas classics such as these.
— *Fried asparagus, ham, and cheese bundles* 52
— *Eggplant and cheese fritters* 31
— *Ham croquettes* 55

Esteban Miñana, Valencia

La Bodeguilla del Gato is among Valencia's favorite nocturnal haunts in groovy El Carmen, serving Esteban's tasty tapas.
— *Fishermen's mussels* 106
— *Spicy sausage in red wine* 60
— *Squid in a tomato, garlic, and red wine sauce* 121

María Agustina Ostiz, Pamplona

María Agustina, who trained under Juan Mari Arzak, devised these pintxo recipes while working at Pamplona's award-winning bar and restaurant, Baserri.
— *Fried zucchini, shrimp, and bacon bundles* 85
— *Smoked cod, tomato, and black-olive oil toasts* 84
— *Smoked salmon, anchovy, and red pepper toasts* 83

Miguel Reguera García, Salamanca

When Miguel opened Momo, it took Salamanca by storm, bringing designer pintxos to a conservative, essentially Renaissance town.
— *Cream cheese and leek toasts* 32
— *Foie gras, zucchini, and bitter orange toasts* 42
— *Ham, artichoke, fava bean, and alioli toasts* 56
— *Ham, fava bean, smoked salmon, and alioli toasts* 57
— *Red pepper, leek, anchovy and cream cheese tarts* 94

José Luis Ruiz Solaguren, Madrid

José Luis, originally Basque and now in his eighties, is Madrid's king of tapas. Owning no fewer than 10 taverns and two restaurants, he is responsible for raising pintxos to a higher level in the capital.
— *Anchovy and sheep cheese on toast* 103
— *Organic cured beef, caviar, or smoked salmon on toast* 103
— *Smoked fish tartar* 104

José María Ruiz, Segovia

King Juan Carlos himself has frequented José Maria's landmark restaurant, which remains totally dedicated to the produce of Castile, including such delicacies as suckling pig.
— *Leeks with summer vegetable vinaigrette* 15
— *Sautéed pork liver with mushrooms and pine nuts* 76
— *Traditional fried Segovian pork and potato* 51

Raquel Sabater, Alicante

Granddaughter of the founder of one of Alicante's oldest tapas bars, Mesón de Labradores, Raquel loves old-style tapas such as these.
— *Fava bean, ham, and sausage stew* 66
— *Poor man's potatoes* 16
— *Spicy pork kabobs* 63

José Angel Valladeres, Paloma Tatay, Andrés Goméz & Fernando Estrada, Madrid

In 1995 four friends took over a peeling tavern, named it Astur, and set about introducing Spain's rural delicacies to local palates. The formula worked and these recipes show why.
— *Lamb stew* 58
— *Mushrooms in parsley sauce* 25
— *Mussels in spicy sauce* 98
— *Red peppers stuffed with blood sausage* 53

Colin Ward, Valencia

A Londoner who grew up in Andalucia, Colin Ward first came to Valencia with a rock n' roll band. As a cook, he excelled at the city's Mediterranean classics as well as recipes from his Mallorcan wife.
— *Cod, spinach, and tomato paella* 80
— *Marinated mackerel with roasted vegetables* 109
— *Squid in tomato, garlic, and red wine sauce* 121

Lourdes Ybarra, Seville

While working as head cook at the ever-popular Bar Europa in Seville, Lourdes helped to establish these typical Andaluz dishes on the city's legendary tapas map.
— *Chilled almond soup* 23
— *Ratatouille with quail eggs* 24
— *Salt cod and orange salad* 116

Manuel Zamora, Seville

Using local ingredients, this ebullient, self-taught cook brought great fantasy to Seville's Bodeguita Casablanca, known as a temple for discerning tapas-hunters.
— *Andalucian-style spinach with chickpeas* 17
— *Chicken legs with prunes and nuts in a blackberry sauce* 69
— *Potato tortilla with whisky sauce* 28
— *Seasoned mashed potatoes* 18
— *Seafood pasta* 111

INDEX

ACKNOWLEDGMENTS

I would like to thank the chefs and bar-owners featured in this book for responding so positively to my requests, collaborating with such good humor and feeding my stomach and soul so magnificently. I am also grateful to the following for their help and advice: Francoçe Butscher at Turmadrid; José Ferri at the Valencia Region Tourist Board; the San Sebastián Convention Bureau; María José Sevilla at the Spanish Embassy, London; Pilar Faro; Mar Mateo; Christopher Branton; Tamsyn Hill; Tim O'Grady; Lorna Scott-Fox and, not least, our recipe translator, Ana Sims, who succeeded with humor in the face of sometimes daunting odds. I would also like to stress my gratitude to the photographer, Jan Baldwin, who sailed through the shoots with immense serenity and humor. Thanks also to Diane Henry for her recipe-testing, to Becca Spry who originally commissioned this book, to Alison Starling for reviving it, and to Jo Wilson for seeing through this new revised version.

GLOSSARY

aceite de oliva—a blend of refined and virgin olive oils with far less flavor than virgin olive oil. The basic olive oil for frying.

aceite de oliva virgen—virgin olive oil with acidity levels up to four percent, quite mild in flavor.

aceite de oliva virgen extra (*primera presión*)—extra-virgin olive oil (first cold pressing) with an acidity level below one percent and a distinctive flavor. Ideal for dressings and drizzles.

aioli—similar to mayonnaise, theoretically without the egg yolk, this Catalan sauce is made from garlic, salt, oil, and optional lemon juice. It is, however, hard to make without the yolk.

anchoas—fresh anchovies or salted anchovy fillets in oil.

bacalao—confusingly, the Spanish word refers both to fresh cod and, far more commonly, to salt cod. The latter form is omnipresent throughout the country and comes in numerous qualities, dependent on their origin.

boquerones—anchovies that are pickled in a wine vinegar.

butifarra—mildly peppered Catalan pork sausage, white or black in color, sometimes including breadcrumbs and with a finer texture than *morcilla*.

cecina—cured beef, typical of León in Old Castile, where it is salted, smoked, and cured. Originally made from horse meat, it is served very finely sliced.

chorizo—spicy cooked sausage flavored with paprika, salt, pepper, and garlic. It comes in fresh, smoked, or cured versions. The best is ninety-five percent pork.

embutidos—a generic term for sausage meats, whether cured, cooked, or fresh.

escabeche—pickling brine or marinade, usually made of oil, vinegar, peppercorns, bay leaves, and/or spices.

guindilla—the chili pepper, which is a New World import to Spain, plays a major role in Spanish cooking. Larger ones are generally milder than smaller ones and the hottest are the dried variety. Red chilies (ripened green chilies) have a sweeter flavor.

jamón ibérico—cured ham from Iberian black-coated pigs.

jamón ibérico de bellota—Spain's top cured ham from black-coated pigs fed on acorns in the wild.

jamón serrano—literally "sawn ham": mass-produced and cured, it is similar to prosciutto, and often used in cooked dishes, when it is more thickly sliced.

jamón de York—cured and cooked ham.

morcilla—the Spanish version of blood sausage (made from pig's blood), which may contain pine nuts and/or rice. The best is from Burgos in Old Castile.

Pedro Ximénez—a very sweet sherry often used in cooking.

pil-pil—a garlic and olive oil sauce that is sometimes made green by the addition of parsley (*salsa verde*).

pimentón (paprika)—the Spanish have two types: *pimentón de la vera* (from Extremadura), a smoked paprika that comes in hot, sweet, and sweet-sour varieties; and straightforward *pimentón*, sun-dried paprika, also in hot and sweet versions and made in Murcia.

pimientos del piquillo—small red peppers, oozing with sweetness and flavor, often found canned, as they are only grown in Navarra.

pintxo—canapé-style tapas, originally from the Basque region.

pisto—originally from La Mancha, a more condensed version of ratatouille made from fried peppers, onion, tomato, garlic, zucchini, eggplant.

raciónes—slightly larger portions than tapas.

requesón—a fresh cheese that is similar to ricotta or cottage cheese.

ventresca de atún bonito—the belly of the tuna fish, regarded as the most tender part and therefore the most sought after. Also found in canned versions at specialty supermarkets.

vinagre—Spaniards use only wine or sherry vinegar, usually red.